GEARED FOR GROWTH BIBLE STUDIES

THE TRINITY

UNDERSTANDING MORE ABOUT GOD, JESUS AND THE HOLY SPIRIT

BIBLE STUDIES TO IMPACT THE LIVES OF ORDINARY PEOPLE

Written by Carol Jones

The Word Worldwide

CHRISTIAN
FOCUS

For details of our titles visit us on our website
www.christianfocus.com

ISBN 978-1-5271-0270-5

Copyright © WEC International

Published in 2018

Christian Focus Publications Ltd.
Geanies House, Fearn, Ross-shire,
IV20 1TW, Scotland, UK
www.christianfocus.com
and
WEC International, The Scala, 115a Far Gosford Street,
Coventry, CV1 5EA, United Kingdom
www.wecinternational.org

Cover design by Daniel van Straaten

Printed by Ashford Colour Press

CONTENTS

QUESTIONS AND NOTES

ANSWER GUIDE

'Where there's LIFE there's GROWTH:
Where there's GROWTH there's LIFE.'

WHY GROW a group?

Because as we study the Bible and share together we can

- Learn to combat loneliness, depression, staleness, frustration, and other problems
- Get to understand and love one another
- Become responsive to the Holy Spirit's dealing and obedient to God's Word

and that's GROWTH.

How do you GROW a group?

- Just start by asking one friend to join you and then aim at expanding your group.
- Study the set portions daily, they are brief and easy: no catches.
- Meet once a week to discuss what you find.
- Befriend others, and work away together

see how it GROWS!

WHEN you GROW ...

Things will happen at school, at home, at work, in your youth group, your student fellowship, women's meetings, midweek meetings, churches, communities and so on.

WHEN you PRAY ...

Remember those involved in the writing and production of these study courses. Pray for groups studying that each member will not only be enriched personally, but will be reaching out continually to involve others. Pray for group leaders and those who direct the studies locally, nationally and internationally.

WHEN you PAY ...

Realise that all profits from the sale of studies go to develop the ministry and have the joy of knowing you are working together with us in the task.

For details of our titles visit us on our websites:
www.christianfocus.com   www.gearedforgrowth.co.uk

ISBN 1-84550-020-2   Copyright ©WEC International   10 9 8 7 6 5 4 3 2 1

INTRODUCTORY STUDY

The Bible is true! It is not a myth. Today we will examine the overwhelming evidence to prove that we can rely on its truths.

Matthew 22:37 tells us to love the Lord with our heart, soul and mind. God has created our minds, so belief in Him is not a blind leap into the dark.

Manuscript Evidence

Today there are in existence over 24,000 manuscript copies of portions of the Old and New Testaments. This is unique in itself because no other documents of this age can even begin to approach such a number.

The Old Testament manuscripts were carefully copied letter by letter, not word by word; all these letters had to balance with the older manuscript so keeping the accuracy of the Bible. Many of these old manuscripts were destroyed, but in 1947 a young Bedouin shepherd boy, looking for his lost goat, found the Dead Sea Scrolls. Many portions of the Old Testament were found here including the book of Isaiah.

Historical Evidence

Was Jesus a real person? Many historians of His time wrote about Him. One of these historians, Josephus, born in A.D. 37, writes about Jesus being a wise man and a doer of wonderful works, that He was condemned to death on the cross by Pilate and was raised from the dead.

Other historians spoke of the darkness which fell when Christ died. Many people were puzzled by the phenomenon and could not find a reasonable explanation for it. It was, however, agreed that it was not an eclipse of the sun.

The Encyclopaedia Britannica states that there is no doubt about the historical evidence of Jesus' existence. Even His opponents wrote of Him.

Prophetical Evidence

There are many Old Testament prophecies that were fulfilled in the New Testament e.g. Micah 5:2 says, *'But you, Bethlehem Ephrathah, though you are small among the clans of Judah, out of you will come for me one who will be ruler over Israel, whose origins are from of old, from ancient times.'* Matthew, in his Gospel (2:6) confirms the fulfilment of Micah's prophecy. Micah prophesied in which Bethlehem Jesus was to be born; for there were two places called Bethlehem, one within seven miles of Nazareth and the other in Judea. Bethlehem Ephrathah in the Old Testament is Bethlehem of Judea in the New Testament.

Other examples of Old and New Testament prophecies that have been or are being fulfilled are:

Zechariah 9:9 *'Rejoice greatly, O Daughter of Zion! Shout! Daughter of Jerusalem!...'*
Now turn to Matthew 21:5 to see the fulfilment of this prophecy.

Isaiah 53 was written 600 years before Jesus was born but was fulfilled in Him.

Leviticus 26:31-33 foretells the destruction of the Temple and the total dispersion of the Jews. The Temple was destroyed in A.D. 70; the dispersion of the Jews and the taking over of the land by the Gentiles took place in A.D. 135; in A.D. 1927 Palestine was described as a land of ruin like no other place.

Ezekiel 36:33-38 records: *'This is what the Sovereign Lord says...'* For almost 2000 years, the Jewish peoples had been scattered throughout the world but they never forgot their culture or desire to return to their own land. In 1948, more than 1 million Jews returned to Israel. They rebuilt the country and farmed the land. Today, Israel is a major exporter of fruit.

Jeremiah 16:14, 15 which reads: *'However, the days are coming...'* is being fulfilled in our own day.

We could quote many other examples of Biblical prophecies that are being fulfilled, but these are enough to affirm that the Bible is the Word of God.

STUDY 1

GOD IS OUR CREATOR

QUESTIONS

DAY 1 *Hebrews 11:3; Psalm 33:6.*
a) How did God create the universe?

b) What material did He use?

DAY 2 *Psalm 90:2; 1 Timothy 1:17; Habakkuk 2:18, 19.*
a) From these verses how do we know that God was not a created being?

b) What is the difference between idols and God?

DAY 3 *Genesis 1:26; 1 Corinthians 8:6; Job 33:4.*
a) Who are the 'we' and 'us' referred to in these scriptures?

b) Think about these verses and discuss your findings.

DAY 4 *Genesis 1:27; Psalm 145:18.*
a) In whose likeness was man made?

b) In what way can we draw near to God?

DAY 5 *Isaiah 45:18; Psalm 104:13, 14.*

a) Why did God create His wonderful world?

b) How does God continually provide for man, animals and birds?

DAY 6 *Genesis 2:18-24; Genesis 1:27, 28.*

a) Why did God create a woman out of a man's rib?

b) Why did God make a man and a woman?

DAY 7 *Romans 1:20; Acts 14:17; Psalm 19:1.*

a) Why is the unbeliever without excuse?

b) List the evidence God has given us of His existence.

c) How does creation make you feel about God?

NOTES

Where did life begin?

God has given us His answer in Genesis chapter 1. The word Genesis actually means 'origin' and this book tells us how God created the universe and the human race. For many years men have sought to explain away the Bible's account of creation, creating scientific theories of the origin of life. In the Bible we see that God created the world, an amazing world suitable for us to live in. He has provided all we need to live on earth. He has positioned the earth perfectly in the universe. If we were too near to the sun we would burn, if we were too far from the sun we would freeze. God has accurately put the earth in place. *'He spreads out the northern skies over empty space; he suspends the earth over nothing'* (Job 26:7).

He also created different kinds of fish, birds and animals. Some may have become extinct, e.g. dinosaurs, and others will have adapted to their different environment, but they are still fish, birds and animals just as God created them. *'All flesh is not the same: Men have one kind of flesh, animals have another, birds another and fish another'* (1 Cor. 15:39).

It is also interesting to note that in His creation God made adult plants, trees and creatures. He didn't just plant the seeds or create the eggs. What He created was made to produce seed and reproduce their species. 'Then God said, *"Let the land produce vegetation: seed-bearing plants and trees on the land that bear fruit with seed in it, according to their various kinds".'* (Gen. 1:11). Genesis 1:20-23 gives another example. God created an adult man and woman. When He created our world it was a mature world, that is, it had an appearance of age just as the plants, animals and man had, although it was only a few days old. This is why scientifically the age of the earth cannot be measured. When you are told that God did not create the world, that science has disproved the Bible, don't believe it. God has given us a complete account of how He created the universe and everything in it. When we see creation around us we know that this cannot be an accident but the work of our Mighty Creator.

How many of us have ever sat down and thought about the wonders of our world? Even the air we breathe is amazing, it only covers the earth with a fine film, and the higher you go the thinner the oxygen gets. He has provided everything we need to sustain life on earth.

STUDY 2

GOD IS ...

QUESTIONS

DAY 1 *Matthew 7:9-11; Galatians 3:26; John 1:10-13.*

    a) What difference is shown between earthly fathers and God?

    b) Are all people born as children of God?

    c) How do we become God's children?

DAY 2 *John 3:16; Romans 5:8; Isaiah 53:6*

    a) In what way has God shown us how much He loves us?

    b) Why don't we deserve God's love?

DAY 3 *Titus 3:5; 1 John 1:9; Ephesians 2:4, 5.*

    a) As seen in these verses what are the characteristics of God that allow us to come to Him?

    b) Should your failures prevent you from coming to God?

    c) What effect does God's mercy have on your life?

QUESTIONS (contd.)

DAY 4 *I Kings 8:56; Deuteronomy 7:9.*
    a) Why can we trust God absolutely?

    b) How does the faithfulness of God affect your life?

DAY 5 *Titus 1:1-3; Hebrews 6:18, 19.*
    a) What is the difference between humans and God in these verses?

    b) List the positive results of knowing that God is true and cannot lie.

DAY 6 *Hebrews 4:13; Psalm 139:2-6.*
    a) What can be hidden from God?

    b) What can God see that man cannot see?

DAY 7 *Deuteronomy 32:4; Malachi 3:5; Romans 2:1, 2.*
    a) What does God tell us about His justice?

    b) From these verses what do you think makes God a just judge?

    c) When you have been wrongly judged, how have you reacted?

NOTES

Every day we have studied a different characteristic of God.

God is our Father

What a wonderful, close relationship this is! The followers of no other religion call their god 'father'. It is unique to the Christian faith. To become a true child of God we must receive His Son Jesus into our lives. *'He came to that which was his own, but his own did not receive him. Yet to all who received him, to those who believed in his name, he gave the right to become children of God – children born not of natural descent nor of human decision or a husband's will, but born of God'* (John 1:11-13). Then we can call God our Father. Some of us have had earthly fathers who may have abused us, deserted us or been unfair to us. This is why we need to see that our Father God is so different!

God is love

Think about this: God is love. The word 'love' has been batted around in our world today until people hardly know what it means to love or to be loved. God's love is true. He doesn't say He loves us today and forgets us tomorrow. God means what He says, we can depend on that. God loves us even when we don't deserve it. There are times when we feel that we deserve to be loved by others and yet don't receive that love, e.g. we may have been good wives, husbands, parents, children or friends and yet, been rejected. Perhaps this is how God feels when we don't return His love.

God is merciful and forgiving

I wonder what comes to your mind when you think of mercy. The word 'mercy' reminds me of a man crying for mercy from a cruel torturer who delights in the cries of the poor man. God's mercy and God's forgiveness are not like that. He does not delight in our anguish and pain but is waiting to extend His hand of mercy to us. His love to us is shown in His mercy and forgiveness... *'If you, O Lord, kept a record of sins, O Lord, who could stand? But with you there is forgiveness; therefore you are feared'* (Ps. 130:3, 4).

God is faithful and keeps His promises

When we make promises we usually mean to keep them but, unfortunately, we cannot always do so. When God makes promises He is true to His Word and always keeps His promises. There is no fear in trusting God because He is faithful.

God is truth and cannot lie

Our study shows us that it is impossible for God to lie. Sometimes this can be hard to take in as we live in a world where lies are normal. The devil is the father of lies.

Although we are surrounded by these things we can believe in God who cannot lie, and we can put our whole trust in Him.

God knows everything

If we have a close relationship with God and are completely open before Him, hiding nothing, we will know His blessing on our lives as we realise God has a personal knowledge of us.

The opposite can be frightening. We think we can hide from God but we cannot. We can pretend before people but we cannot pretend before God. We can fool people but we cannot fool God; He knows everything about us.

God is a just Judge

Many people have experienced injustice in our world ranging from an innocent man condemned to death to the child who sees that he is unfairly treated. It can be difficult to judge when faced with convincing people who claim their innocence when they are guilty. In many parts of our world today those who have no understanding of justice treat people unjustly. However, our God is a just Judge and will judge all men fairly.

STUDY 3

GOD IS ...

QUESTIONS

DAY 1 *Isaiah 6:1-8; Revelation 15:3-4.*

a) What were the creatures crying?

b) Who alone is holy?

DAY 2 *1 Chronicles 29:10-13; Revelation 19:6.*

a) From these verses list all the attributes of God.

b) In your own words what comes to mind when you think of God as King?

c) What should our attitude be towards Him as King?

DAY 3 *1 Kings 8:10,11; 1 Timothy 6:16; Luke 2:9.*

a) What words are used to describe the presence of the Lord in these verses?

b) What effect did the glory of the Lord's presence have on men?

DAY 4 *Matthew 19:26; Ephesians 3:20; Isaiah 43:13.*

a) How is God's power shown in these verses?

b) How can God solve our difficulty or problem?

DAY 5 *Psalm 139:7-10; Jeremiah 23:23, 24; Psalm 145:18.*
  a) Where is God?

b) Why can't we escape from God?

c) How do we get near to God?

DAY 6 *Psalm 102:25-27; Malachi 3:6.*
  a) What will change and who is always the same?

b) What statement do we find in the Malachi reading?

DAY 7 *Isaiah 57:15; Psalm 9:7; Deuteronomy 33:27.*
  a) What aspects of God are shown in these verses?

b) What promise can we claim from Deuteronomy 33:27?

NOTES

This week we have studied a further seven characteristics of God.

God is holy
The *Oxford English Dictionary* tells us that the word 'holy' means morally and spiritually perfect. God is perfect and pure in all His ways. When Isaiah saw the Lord he also saw himself and said, 'There is no hope for me.' The holiness of the Lord was dazzling and showed up his human sinfulness. It is important to realise that God is holy. This will help us to treat Him with reverence.

God is sovereign
This means that God is King, supreme ruler over all, that nothing is out of His control. In past centuries in Eastern civilisations, it would have been certain death for any person, including the queen, to approach the king without his personal invitation to do so. If a man who is a king, has such power and authority, how much more power and authority belongs to our 'Heavenly King.'

God is glorious
God lives in the light that no one can approach. This is the description of His glory, a shining, a dazzling light. The holiness and sovereignty of God are shown in His glory. We see the effect His glory had upon man. Today if we had just a glimpse of His glory we would never be the same again.

God is powerful
God's power is immeasurable; He alone is all-powerful. Imagine such power in evil hands – this would be unthinkable. Our God is holy, He is love, He is truth, He is just and all authority is His.

God is everywhere (omnipresent)
It can be difficult for our minds to take in that God is everywhere and there is no place where we can hide from Him. Many people have tried to run away from God or from the influence of a godly home, only to find that they cannot escape from God's presence. Deanna knew that the Lord was speaking to her but she didn't want to listen to what He had to say. She thought the best thing she could do was to fly away to New Zealand and away from God, but she found He was there as well and continued to speak to her. This time Deanna heard what God was saying and responded to His call upon her life to serve Him wherever He wanted her to go. He brought her back to England to work for Him and in His time she returned to New Zealand to serve Him there. It is a comfort to know that because God is everywhere, He is only a prayer away.

God is unchangeable
Do you know a moody person? Can you imagine living with a person who changes his or her mind and mood with the weather? You never know the reaction of such people. How good it is to know that God is always the same. What He says He means; His

love for us is constant; His Word is true; He keeps His promises. We know that He is always there for us and will never leave us or abandon us. *'Jesus Christ is the same yesterday, today and forever'* (Heb. 13:8).

God is eternal

I remember being asked the question when I taught children in Sunday school, 'Who made God?' To explain that God was not made but that He always has been and always will be, can be difficult for us to understand. The fact is we can never understand God because He is God and we are human beings. God has no beginning or ending: *'I am the Alpha and the Omega, says the Lord God, who is and who was, and who is to come, the Almighty'* (Rev. 1:8). The opening words of the Bible are, *'In the beginning, God...'* and you cannot go any further back than that.

STUDY 4

JESUS IS ...

QUESTIONS

DAY 1 *John 1:1-3, 14; Proverbs 8:22-31.*

a) Who is known as the Word?

b) What do these verses tell us about Jesus?

DAY 2 *Luke 1:26-38; Matthew 1:18.*

a) What important message did Gabriel have for Mary?

b) Why did Mary question the angel Gabriel?

c) What was Gabriel's answer to her question?

d) What was Mary's reply and how would the cost of the reply affect her?

DAY 3 *Luke 2:41-52.*

a) Why did Jesus amaze the Jewish teachers?

b) What reactions did Mary experience?

c) Who did Jesus call Father?

DAY 4 *Mark 1:9-11; Matthew 17:5; John 2:5.*

a) Yesterday we saw that Jesus, even as a boy, knew He was God's Son. How does God the Father confirm this in today's verses?

QUESTIONS (contd.)

b) What important instruction does God give His disciples?

c) How can this apply to us today?

DAY 5 *Mark 1:12, 13; Hebrews 2:18; Hebrews 4:14-16.*
a) Did Jesus sin when He was tempted?

b) Why does Jesus understand our temptations?

c) What should we do when we are going through temptation?

DAY 6 *Matthew 4:18-22; Matthew 9:9, 10; Luke 18:28-30; Luke 19:1-9.*
a) What were these men doing when Jesus called them?

b) Because Matthew was a tax collector, how did the people treat him?

c) Why is it costly for you to follow Jesus?

DAY 7 *John 7:14-16; Mark 4:33,34; Luke 15:8-10.*
a) The Jewish authorities taught the law, but what was the teaching of Jesus?

b) Luke 15:8-10 is a parable. Why did Jesus teach in parables?

NOTES

This week we have studied what the Bible teaches about Jesus.

Jesus is God

We see from the scriptures that the Word became a human being. Colossians 2:9, 10 are important verses that show us that Jesus is God. Jesus was not created because He was there when the world was created. We read from the gospels of Matthew and Luke about the Word becoming a human being. Reading both accounts gives us a full story of all that happened at the birth of Jesus.

Jesus is the Son of God

Mary was a virgin, so the conception of Jesus in her womb was a miracle. Can you imagine how she felt when the angel gave her the news? Her feelings would have been mixed. On the one hand she would have been delighted with such an honour, but on the other, been fearful of the consequences. Who would believe her? The punishment for having a child outside of marriage was stoning! Her acceptance of the angel's message was amazing.

As Jesus grew it was evident that He was God's Son; even the Jewish teachers were astounded at His knowledge when He was just a boy. Jesus knew who He was; He called God His Father. Later on in His life, at His baptism, God calls Him His Son. The Jewish authorities were determined to kill Him because He called God His Father.

Jesus is tempted

After baptism, Satan tempted Jesus. It is interesting to read that Jesus always answered Satan with a verse from the scriptures. Get to know your Bible and it will be a real help when Satan tempts you. Remember, Jesus understands all the temptations we go through and we can call upon Him and He will make a way of escape for us.

Jesus calls us

I really love the thought that Jesus calls ordinary people to be His followers. We may have been left out by the world's standards, but Jesus calls us to follow Him. Jesus chose, as His followers, people from all walks of life. The four fishermen He called were ordinary men with no education, Matthew was a tax collector and Luke was a doctor. It really didn't matter, Jesus called them because He knew their hearts.

Jesus is the greatest Teacher

How did Jesus teach? He often used parables. What is a parable? It's an earthly story with a heavenly meaning. We usually remember stories and the full meaning of the message is shown clearly in a story of everyday life.

STUDY 5

QUESTIONS

DAY 1 *John 2:1-11; Luke 19:5-9; Matthew 8:14, 15.*

    a) What difference did Jesus make when He became a guest?

    b) These people had problems. Do you have problems in your home or life?

    c) If Jesus is the same today, how is He able to help with our problems?

DAY 2 *Matthew 14:15-21; Luke 8:22-25.*

    a) Here are two accounts of the miracles of Jesus. What is a miracle?

    b) What part did the disciples play in the feeding of the people?

    c) How did the disciples react and what question did they ask one another?

DAY 3 *Matthew 8:2, 3; Matthew 15:30, 31; Matthew 11:2-6.*

    a) How did Jesus answer the statement, 'If you want to, you can make me clean'?

    b) How would you answer the question asked by John the Baptist?

    c) Many needs are brought to Jesus in these verses. Add your own needs to them and lay your requests at His feet.

DAY 4 *John 11:1-46.*

    a) Why did Jesus wait two days before going to Lazarus?

QUESTIONS (contd.)

b) Why was Mary disappointed when Jesus arrived late? How would you have felt in her situation?

c) What were the differing reactions of those who saw Jesus raise Lazarus from the dead?

DAY 5 *John 8:3-11; Psalms 51:3, 10.*
a) Why did the Pharisees bring the adulterous woman to Jesus?

b) Why did they all leave?

c) Jesus did not condemn the woman, but what warning did He give her?

DAY 6 *Mark 10:17-22; Matthew 6:19-21.*
a) What can this young man be commended for?

b) What hindered this man from following Jesus?

c) Ask yourself the question, 'Who or what do I love most'?

DAY 7 *Matthew 26:6-13; I Peter 1:8,9.*
a) How did the reactions of Jesus and the disciples differ towards the woman?

b) How did the woman express her love for Jesus?

c) In our own lives what counts more, is it God's approval or man's?

Jesus is the Miracle-Worker

Jesus made a difference to every life He touched and this week we meet some of the people with whom He came into contact. We begin with Jesus as a guest at a wedding. Have you ever been to a wedding where things have gone wrong? I'm sure you have. When my friend got married the best man was late! Of course he had the ring, so they had to borrow the vicar's wedding ring in order to get married. We can laugh at these things but I am sure they were not laughing in the wedding at Cana when the wine ran out. Here Jesus performed His first miracle, turning water into the very best wine. We also see Him as a guest in the home of Zacchaeus where He completely changed this man's way of life; when He visited Peter's house He brought healing. My father worked with a man who was a Christian. Some of the men were mocking him and saying, *'How can you say that Jesus turned water into wine?'* The man answered, *'I know that he changed beer into furniture in my home.'* When invited, Jesus makes the difference.

Jesus is Sovereign

Jesus touched many lives when He fed the 5,000 men plus women and children with five loaves and two fish. They were all witnesses to this great miracle. He surprised His disciples when He calmed the storm as most of these men were seasoned fishermen used to stormy Galilee, but during the storm they feared for their lives. Jesus has complete control over storms whether at sea or in our lives.

Jesus is the giver of life

When the man suffering from leprosy came to Jesus he said, *'Sir, if you want to, you can make me clean.'* Jesus stretched out his hand and touched him. *'I do want to,'* He answered. *'Be clean!'* (Matt. 8:2,3 GNB). Jesus shows His compassion for this man and to those who were brought to Him. When Jesus visited Lazarus it was at his tomb. Mary and Martha must have thought that Jesus didn't care, because in their minds He came too late, Lazarus was already dead. It's incredible that after seeing Lazarus raised from the dead and with many people believing in Jesus, some of the leaders began to make plans to kill Him.

Jesus is merciful

I am sure that the woman caught in adultery was grateful she met Jesus that day. In the hands of those who brought her to Jesus she would have been stoned to death. Jesus had such a wonderful way of answering those who were trying to trap Him. In this case they all knew they were not innocent, so could not pick up the first stone and throw it at the woman. The Lord's forgiveness and mercy are seen clearly in this account.

Jesus is all-knowing

When Jesus spoke to the rich young man, He put His finger on the hindrance in his life. The gloom that spread over the man's face when Jesus told him to give all his money to the poor, shows us this man's love for his money. In complete contrast, the woman who poured expensive perfume on the head of Jesus showed how much she loved Jesus. Note how she was criticised for this act of devotion. When we give our lives wholeheartedly to the Lord we may not have man's approval but remember it's not what men say about us, it's what God knows about us that counts.

STUDY 6

THE WEEK PRIOR TO THE DEATH OF JESUS

QUESTIONS

DAY 1 *John 12:12-16; Luke 19:30; Zechariah 9:9.*

a) How did the people react to Jesus when He came into Jerusalem?

b) What is significant about the mode of transport Jesus used?

c) When did the disciples remember what Zechariah had prophesied about Jesus?

DAY 2 *Matthew 21:12,13; John 2:17.*

a) What did God say the temple should be called?

b) How was the temple being used and what had it become?

c) Why did Jesus drive the merchants and money changers out of the temple?

DAY3 *Luke 21:1-4; 2 Corinthians 9:6,7; Luke 6:38.*

a) How could Jesus say that the poor woman had put in more than all the others?

b) What guidelines and promises on giving do we have from these scriptures?

c) What else can I give besides money that will bring blessing to others and myself?

DAY 4 *Matthew 26:26-28; 1 Corinthians 11:23-29.*

a) What is the meaning of the bread and wine?

b) Why is it important to recognise the meaning of eating the bread and drinking the wine?

c) What should we do before eating the Lord's Supper?

DAY 5 *John 13:4-17; Matthew 20:25-28.*

a) Why were the disciples shocked when Jesus started to wash their feet?

b) How does this act and teaching of Jesus affect our lives today?

DAY 6 *Matthew 26:36-39; Luke 22:43,44; Luke 23:33.*

a) What did Jesus mean when He prayed for the cup to be taken from Him?

b) How did the anguish and sorrow of Jesus show?

c) In the face of such anguish and the complete obedience to His Father, can I say in my difficult circumstances, 'Not my will but yours be done'?

DAY 7 *Matthew 26:14-16; Luke 22:47,48; Matthew 27:3-5.*

a) What did the love of money tempt Judas to do?

b) Judas betrayed Jesus with a kiss. In what way do I betray Jesus?

c) When Jesus was condemned, what did Judas think of the money?

Jesus is the One Who fulfilled prophecy

The week prior to His death, Jesus knew that this was to be His last week before His arrest and crucifixion. Imagine if you knew you had only one week left to live, how would you spend that week? Doing things you needed to do, or visiting those you love? Getting your house in order, saying sorry to people you had hurt, telling people you had never told how much you appreciated them? Perhaps telling others of your love for God and assurance of heaven. All that was written of Jesus in the scriptures would be fulfilled. The Lord Jesus too had work to do and important things to say during His last week.

Jesus is King

The first thing Jesus did was to humbly enter Jerusalem, riding on a colt. It was the Passover and Jerusalem would have been overflowing with people. His coming to Jerusalem was dramatic: everyone knew He had arrived. Jesus entered the temple and drove out the traders who were making His Father's house a den of thieves. Jesus was fearless and showed His authority.

Jesus is all-seeing (Omniscient)

Jesus also sees the most insignificant people; He saw the poor widow giving all she had into the treasury. We never lose out when we give to God. You can never 'out give' God because He always gives you so much more in return.

Jesus is the Passover Lamb

Arrangements are made at the end of the week to celebrate the Passover together. Jesus sits at the table with His disciples and symbolically breaks the bread and distributes it along with the wine. He is teaching His disciples to eat the bread and drink the wine, and as often as they do this they will remember His death. Jesus was still with them, but He would die very soon and then they would remember the importance of the Lord's Supper.

Jesus is the humble servant

At this meal Jesus gives them an example of humility by washing their feet, a task only servants performed. After the meal Jesus went with His disciples to Gethsemane where He prayed to His Father in agony knowing what was to come and the great cost He had to pay to gain salvation for the world.

Jesus chose His Father's will

When He had finished praying, His betrayer, Judas, came with a crowd to arrest Him. Jesus knew that Judas would betray Him. Judas, one of the twelve disciples, was the treasurer, but also a thief, and Jesus knew this. It is so sad that this man listened to Satan and was tempted to betray Jesus for 30 pieces of silver, the price of a slave.

STUDY 7

JESUS, HIS COMPLETED WORK

QUESTIONS

DAY 1 *Matthew 26:33-35; Luke 22:54-62.*

    a) Peter was strong when he proclaimed his undying allegiance to Jesus. What caused him to deny Him now?

    b) What effect did the Lord's look have on Peter?

    c) Can we identify with Peter here? Share your own experiences.

DAY 2 *Matthew 27:1,2; John 18:38-40; Matthew 27:23,24.*

    a) Who was Pilate?

    b) What choice did the people make?

    c) Why did Pilate wash his hands? Do you think he could wash away his responsibility? Am I in danger of doing a similar thing?

DAY 3 *Matthew 27:27-31; John 19:23, 24; Psalm 22:18.*

    a) What cruel acts did the soldiers perform against Jesus?

    b) What prophecy was fulfilled in these scriptures?

DAY 4 *Mark 15:27; Luke 23:39-43; Acts 2:21.*

    a) What are the similarities and differences between these two criminals?

    b) What promise did Jesus give to the thief? Did he deserve it?

    c) To whom is the promise given?

QUESTIONS (contd.)

DAY 5 *John 19:25-27; John 3:16-18.*

    a) How do you think Mary the mother of Jesus felt as she stood by the cross?

    b) Jesus made provision for His mother. What can this teach us?

    c) Jesus showed His love in action. How should we react?

DAY 6 *Matthew 27:36-54; Luke 23:34.*

    a) What unusual phenomena occurred at the death of Jesus?

    b) Imagine you are one of these soldiers – describe your feelings.

    c) What was the attitude of Jesus towards these soldiers? Ask God to enable you to have the same attitude of forgiveness.

DAY 7 *John 19:38-42; Isaiah 53:8,9.*

    a) Joseph and Nicodemas had been secret followers of Jesus. How did they show their love for Him now?

    b) Isaiah prophesied Jesus' death and burial. Jesus was innocent; why did God allow His death?

    c) Are you a secret follower of Jesus? Do you find it difficult to tell others that Jesus died for your sins?

Jesus knows our hearts

Every day this week we have met different people who were there with Jesus from His arrest right up to His burial. Every person had different feelings towards Him. Some loved Him, some hated Him, others failed Him and there were those who wanted to show they cared for Him against all opposition. They were different people with different attitudes and reactions, people like us. How would we have reacted if we had been there?

Jesus is the One who forgives

We begin with Peter. Can you imagine what Peter felt that day when he saw Jesus being arrested? Normally Peter was very strong, a tough fisherman who never let anything stand in his way. He never thought he could ever deny his Lord, and showed this as he wept bitterly. *'The fear of man will prove to be a snare, but whoever trusts in the Lord is kept safe'* (Prov. 29:25). An animal caught in a snare cannot move in the same way, and if we fear man we will not be able to open our mouths to confess Him. We will be, like Peter, filled with fear.

Jesus is the truth

Pilate had full power over life and death, and could reverse capital sentences passed by the Sanhedrin. His wife had a dream about Jesus and sent a message to Pilate telling him to have nothing to do with Him because He was innocent. Pilate didn't listen to the advice of his wife, and according to Greek historians, he committed suicide a few years later. He could never pass on the responsibility of Jesus' death to others by the washing of his hands.

The soldiers were cruel men and had crucified many others. It seems they made sport of the fact that Jesus claimed to be the Son of God. This amused them, and they mocked Him even more, then sat and watched Him on the cross. What a shock they had and what fear came upon them when the earth shook and the sun withdrew its light when Jesus died. Never had they ever seen such a thing before. The centurion along with the soldiers exclaimed, 'Surely this was the Son of God!'

Jesus is full of compassion

Two thieves were crucified with Jesus and had opposite reactions. One mocked Him and one called to Him. Two people can be in exactly the same situation; one will blame and curse God and the other will call on God for help.

Jesus is our peace

Mary, like the disciples, didn't understand what was happening. Although Jesus was her son, He was also God's Son. How could this be happening? He was being crucified before her very eyes; it seemed that all her hopes were dashed. Sometimes we may feel like Mary. We don't understand why others or ourselves have to suffer. It is enough to know that God understands, and one day, like Mary, we will understand.

Jesus is our courage

We end this week with Joseph and Nicodemus who had been secret disciples of Jesus. Joseph, a member of the Sanhedrin, the highest council of the Jews, had not voted for Jesus' death. Nicodemus was a very important man in Jerusalem. He too was a member of the Sanhedrin, but despite his high position he lost his fear and showed his love and devotion to Jesus by helping with His burial.

STUDY 8

JESUS IS ALIVE

QUESTIONS

DAY 1 *Matthew 27:62-66; Matthew 28:2-4, 11,15.*

a) Why was the tomb sealed and guarded?

b) What did the soldiers witness while on guard?

c) What plan did the chief priests and elders make when they heard the disturbing news from the soldiers?

DAY 2 *Luke 24:1-9; Matthew 16:21.*

a) What question did the angels ask the women?

b) Although Jesus had said He would be raised from the dead, do you think the women expected this? What actions confirmed this?

c) Compare the reaction of the women to the reaction of the guards in yesterday's study.

DAY 3 *Mark 16:7; Luke 24:11,12; 1 Corinthians 15:5,6.*

a) What does the Mark reading show us in the light of Peter's denial of Jesus?

b) Peter may have had doubts, but what did he do?

c) What was the evidence of the resurrection?

DAY 4 *John 20:19,20,24-29; Luke 24:36-43.*

a) Why did the disciples think that Jesus was a ghost?

b) Why did Thomas doubt?

QUESTIONS (contd.)

c) What did Jesus say about seeing and believing?

DAY 5 *Luke 24:13-32.*

Describe the feelings of these two as they walked along the Emmaus road:

a) Before Jesus walked with them.

b) When Jesus walked with them.

c) When they realised who He was.

DAY 6 *I Corinthians 15:3-6; John 6:40; 2 Corinthians 4:14.*

a) What evidence of the resurrection of Jesus Christ is seen here?

b) What are the promises of the Father to those who believe?

c) How can we know we will be raised up with Jesus?

DAY 7 *Luke 24:50-53; Acts 1:9-11.*

a) How did the disciples react to the ascension (Jesus being taken up to heaven)?

b) What message did the men in white (angels) have for the disciples?

c) If Jesus is alive and I believe it, what difference does He make in my life?

Jesus is alive

The chief priests and Pharisees had heard Jesus say that three days after His death He would be raised to life. They arranged to seal the huge stone that had been placed at the entrance of His tomb and to place soldiers on guard. Their excuse: to prevent the followers of Jesus from stealing the body and lying about His resurrection. I wonder if they really thought Jesus would rise from the dead? Remember, many of them had seen Jesus' miracles, and knew that Lazarus and others had been raised from the dead. Imagine the confusion of the Jewish leaders when the soldiers returned with the news that Jesus had indeed been raised to life. Their schemes gave added proof to the resurrection, but to save face, they paid the soldiers to lie about the evidence.

Jesus is our problem-solver

The next group of people were the women who came to anoint His body with spices. As they walked to the tomb they wondered how on earth they would be able to move the stone away. When they arrived their problem had been solved; Jesus had risen from the dead and the stone had already been rolled away. When you compare the reactions of people who have witnessed the same things it's surprising how they differ. The guards were paid to tell lies, but these women went immediately to tell others the good news.

Jesus is our faith

The disciples were full of doubt when the women told them what they had seen, but Peter went immediately to investigate. Peter was a man of action; he didn't just sit down and let everything happen around him but got involved. We read about Peter denying that he knew Jesus, but later we have Jesus reaching out to him by name. Our failures don't disqualify us from serving God because the Lord forgives us and puts us back on our feet. When a small child is learning to walk he doesn't give up at the first fall but gets back onto his feet and tries again.

The disciples were shaken when Jesus suddenly appeared before them in the upper room and thought they had seen a ghost. Jesus clarified this confusion by showing them that He was real, that He was flesh and bone. Thomas doubted because he had not been there and said he would not believe until he saw for himself. We were not there. We have not seen the Lord Jesus in bodily form and yet Jesus encourages us by saying that we are blessed when we believe, even though we have never seen Him.

Jesus is our joy

Meeting the two on the road to Emmaus gives us a good picture of how the followers of Jesus felt. They said, 'We had hoped…' Their hopes had been dashed. Jesus Himself drew near and began to explain to them the purpose of His life and death. Their hearts burned within them as He spoke, and instead of despair they were filled with joy.

Jesus is everlasting life

Yes, we believe Jesus died for our sins and that He rose again from the dead, but how does this affect our lives? What hope does this give us today? It means that believing in Jesus we are forgiven and we too will be raised to life. Our Christian life is not just for now but for eternity.

Jesus is eternal

We finish this week with the account of the ascension when Jesus was taken up to heaven. The disciples all stood around as they watched Him rise up into the sky until a cloud hid Him from their sight. Suddenly two angels appeared to explain that He had been taken to heaven and would return to earth in the same way as they had seen Him go. His return to earth is called the second coming of Christ.

This study does not end with hopelessness, but with hope.

STUDY 9

THE HOLY SPIRIT IS ...

QUESTIONS

DAY 1 *Matthew 28:19, 20; 2 Corinthians 13:14; Luke 4:18; John 15:26.*

a) Which verses show us the unity of the Father, Son and Holy Spirit?

b) Who is the Holy Spirit?

c) What other names are given to the Holy Spirit in John 15:26?

DAY 2 *Acts 2:1-13.*

a) In what way did the Holy Spirit come to those in the upper room?

b) Who witnessed the coming of the Holy Spirit besides the believers?

c) What two different reactions did the people have?

DAY 3 *Ephesians 5:18; 3:16-19; 1 Corinthians 2:4-5.*

a) What are we encouraged to do in these verses?

b) What does our faith rest on?

DAY 4 *1 Corinthians 3:16; 1 Corinthians 6:19-20; Romans 8:9; John 14:15-17.*

a) What do we become when God's Spirit lives in us?

b) What difference does the Holy Spirit make to our daily life?

QUESTIONS (contd.)

DAY 5 *Galatians 5:22, 23; John 15:4,5.*

    a) What is the fruit of the Spirit?

    b) How is the fruit of the Spirit produced in our lives?

    c) How is the fruit expressed in our lives?

DAY 6 *Ephesians 4:11-13; Romans 12:6-8.*

    a) What are the ministry gifts of the Holy Spirit listed in Ephesians 4:11-13?

    b) What gifts can we find in Romans 12:6-8, which are not listed in Ephesians?

    c) Do you have any of these gifts? If so, which gifts do you believe you have received?

DAY 7 *1 Corinthians 12:1-11.*

    a) List the gifts of the Holy Spirit in these verses.

    b) Who gave these gifts and why don't we all have the same gifts?

    c) Are you willing to open up your heart to allow God's Holy Spirit to use you through the gifts He chooses?

NOTES

I trust that by now we know more about God, the Lord Jesus Christ and the Holy Spirit.

God the Holy Spirit

Here we see clearly the unity between God the Father, God the Son and God the Holy Spirit. In the church we use the term, the Trinity. Although we do not find this word in the Bible, we can see the truth of God the Three in One clearly in our studies. God's Holy Spirit enters our lives when we receive Jesus Christ as our personal Saviour and Lord.

The Holy Spirit has come

The day of Pentecost was a special feast day in Jerusalem. It would have been buzzing with excitement as people arrived from many nations to celebrate the feast of Pentecost. The Holy Spirit came suddenly, but not to a sleepy little village where hardly anyone would have noticed, but to a bustling city, full of foreigners. When the Holy Spirit came upon the followers of Jesus, crowds gathered around to see what was happening. Each heard them speaking in their own native language. What a setting for a sermon! Peter addresses the crowd telling them that this was what the prophet Joel had spoken about in Joel 2:28,29: *'I will pour out my Spirit on all people. Your sons and daughters will prophesy, your old men will dream dreams, your young men will see visions. Even on my servants, both men and women, I will pour out my Spirit in those days.'* The Holy Spirit had come upon Peter, who was now filled with power and boldness and proclaimed that God had raised Jesus from the dead, and exalted Him to the right hand of God. Peter and the disciples were all witnesses to this fact.

The filling of the Holy Spirit

In Paul's letter to the Ephesians, we are commanded to be filled with the Holy Spirit, who is the very nature of God. Although I had been a Christian for many years, I had an overwhelming longing for more of God in my life. A few years ago, I prayed and simply asked God for more of Himself. He answered me and filled me with His Holy Spirit. In the *Oxford English Dictionary* the word 'fill' means to make full, to occupy completely. As we open up our lives to the Lord, He will come, occupy and fill those areas we have kept closed to Him. If we do this, there will be less of us in our lives and more of Him.

The Holy Spirit dwells within God's children

The inner sanctuary of the temple in the Old Testament times was the place where the presence of God was, and in 1 Kings 8:10-11 we read how the cloud of God's presence filled the temple of the Lord when the priests withdrew from the Holy Place. The priests could not perform their service because the cloud, the glory of the Lord, filled His temple. In the New Testament we read, *'your body is a temple of the Holy Spirit, who is in you, whom you have received from God'* (1 Cor. 6:19). So, if God's Holy Spirit lives within us, we must make sure that nothing in our lives prevents Him from working through us.

The fruit of the Holy Spirit

How does a tree produce fruit? The tree takes its nourishment through the roots, and the sap rises to the branches where the fruit is produced. The branch has to be attached to the tree before it can bear fruit. In the same way we produce spiritual fruit as we allow the Holy Spirit to flow through our lives. It's not by trying our very best to be joyful, patient, loving and so on, but by being united to the Lord and allowing His life to flow through us.

The Gifts of the Holy Spirit

The Apostle Paul encourages us to desire and set our hearts on spiritual gifts. What is the purpose of these gifts? They are to help, encourage and comfort other people and are used to build up the church. So we can help each other with the gifts that the Holy Spirit gives to us. All the gifts are different and are a God-given ability for us to perform particular tasks.

QUESTIONS

DAY 1 *John 16:7-13.*

a) What is the work of the Holy Spirit as seen in these verses?

b) Are we able to recognise the Holy Spirit working in our lives? Discuss this in your group.

DAY 2 *John 14:16, 17; 16:13-15.*

a) How can we see the Holy Spirit working in these scriptures?

b) How does the Holy Spirit glorify the Lord Jesus Christ?

DAY 3 *Luke 12:11-12; 1 Corinthians 2:12,13.*

a) What promises can we claim for ourselves?

b) How does this affect us?

DAY 4 *Romans 8:26, 27; Ephesians 6:18.*

a) Why do we need the Holy Spirit's help when we pray?

b) Why is it important to be led by the Holy Spirit in our prayers?

QUESTIONS (contd.)

DAY 5 *Acts 13:2-4; 8:26-31.*

    a) What clear guidance does the Holy Spirit give in these passages?

    b) Why did the Holy Spirit guide these men?

    c) Does the Holy Spirit guide in a similar way today? Can you give illustration?

DAY 6 *John 6:63; 10:1-10.*

    a) What kind of life does the Spirit of God give to us?

    b) Compare what God's Spirit gives to that of the thief.

DAY 7 *Acts 7:51; 5:3; Ephesians 4:30; 1 Thessalonians 5:19.*

    a) How do we grieve or make the Holy Spirit sad?

    b) What is God's mark of ownership on each believer?

    c) What should my response be to the Holy Spirit?

Conviction of the Holy Spirit

Remember that the Holy Spirit is in you and He will show you when you have done wrong or grieved Him. This won't be a vague feeling; the Holy Spirit will identify the very thing that is wrong in your life. He is here to guide you, tell you the truth and help you remember all you have learnt about God.

The Holy Spirit is our helper

My youngest daughter has recently come home after working for a year in Romania. What a wonderful help she is to me. I come home from work and find she has washed and ironed the clothes. She has cleaned the house, attic and garage and thrown out all I thought I needed. What a helper! The Holy Spirit is our helper. He is always present with us and, whatever the problem, we can turn to Him for help. He knows exactly what our needs are.

The Holy Spirit is our teacher

The Holy Spirit teaches us what to say; at times our words can be just our own opinion, but the Holy Spirit can give us the right words to speak in any situation. John 14:26 tells us He will help us remember His words to us. He can never help us to remember what we have not read, so read and keep on reading God's Word and He will bring back to our memory the words He wants us to speak to others.

The Holy Spirit's direction in prayer

There are times when we don't know how to pray for a situation, but the Holy Spirit can help us. A few years ago I felt a great burden that filled my heart with anxiety and I knew there were people at that moment who were in very dangerous circumstances. As I was led to pray in the Spirit, I was conscious of the urgency of prayer that God placed upon me. At the same time another person in the prayer meeting had a vision of an aeroplane that was about to crash onto a motorway. In the vision he saw the plane crash on an embankment, missing the motorway and leaving it clear. Later that evening we listened to the news and heard that a passenger aircraft had crashed in England just missing the M1 motorway. The crash had happened when we were praying and the vision that was seen was true. There are times when God, by His Spirit, will direct you to pray into a situation that you do not understand, but others will benefit from your praying.

The leading of the Holy Spirit

When the Holy Spirit leads us to serve Him in different ways it can sometimes be a struggle to obey. Many years ago when we were on holiday I sat on the beach playing with my baby girl. The Lord led me to give a tract to a lady sitting close by with her children but it wasn't easy to do this. Eventually I obeyed the prompting of the Holy Spirit. The woman asked me, 'Why did you give the tract to me and not to another person?' I told her that the Lord had led me to do this. The woman broke down in tears. Her husband had died from cancer a few months earlier and, in her grief, she felt God had forgotten her. The giving of a tract opened the way for a purposeful conversation and now she realised how God had cared for her personally throughout the painful bereavement she had been through. The leading of the Holy Spirit is specific and we need to listen and obey Him when He speaks to us.

The Holy Spirit gives life
I wonder why people think that Christians don't have an enjoyable life. I look around and see people living lives of despair, worry, misery, emptiness, people with blank unhappy faces, and think again of the scripture in John 10:10. *'The thief comes only to steal and kill and destroy; I have come that they may have life, and have it to the full'.* Haven't we experienced that as we reflect on September 11th, 2001? Jesus has sent His Holy Spirit to give us life, not just ordinary mundane life but abundant life.

We can grieve the Holy Spirit
This study ends with a warning. We shouldn't resist God's Holy Spirit, or lie to Him. We shouldn't quench Him when He wants to pour out His Spirit upon us. We should never be afraid of Him; for He is our helper, counsellor and comforter. We are encouraged to let Him have His way in our lives and as we continue to study God's Word, we will see the importance of obeying Him and being led by Him. We will discover how to have a closer walk with God.

'The grace of the Lord Jesus Christ, the love of God, and the fellowship of the Holy Spirit be with you all' (2 Cor. 13:14).

ANSWER GUIDE

The following pages contain an Answer Guide. It is recommended that answers to the questions be attempted before turning to this guide. It is only a guide and the answers given should not be treated as exhaustive.

GUIDE TO STUDY 1

DAY 1 a) By His Word or by His command.

b) God created the earth out of nothing (what cannot be seen).

DAY 2 a) God is eternal. Genesis 1:1 'In the beginning God...' You cannot go further back than the beginning.

b) Man makes idols. God is creator of all things and we worship the God of creation.

DAY 3 a) God the Father, God the Son (Jesus Christ) and God the Holy Spirit.

b) These verses show us that the Father, Son and Holy Spirit (Trinity) created everything. Jesus was not created; He was one with the Father in creation.

DAY 4 a) In God's likeness.

b) We must call to God in sincerity and truth.

DAY 5 a) He made a perfect earth suitable for all of His creation to live on.

b) He provides rain to grow grass for cattle and crops to sustain life.

DAY 6 a) To make a suitable companion for man: one of his kind, bone of his bone and flesh of his flesh.

b) To have children to populate the earth.

DAY 7 a) Because everyone can clearly see God's creation.

b) God has created a perfect world for His creation to live in and has provided everything to sustain life. Even the sky shows His glory.

c) Personal. We have an awesome God! Do we give Him the worship He deserves?

GUIDE TO STUDY 2

DAY 1
a) When God is our heavenly Father and He gives us 'much more'.
b) In the general created sense yes; but as believers, we are 'born anew' and enter into a new relationship with God, a special sonship.
c) Receiving the Lord Jesus Christ by faith.

DAY 2
a) By calling us His children, sending Christ to die for us, not wanting anyone to be destroyed.
b) Because we've turned away from God.

DAY 3
a) God's mercy, forgiveness and grace.
b) Personal. Don't allow your failures to keep you from coming to God because He is merciful.
c) Because by God's mercy we are saved.

DAY 4
a) Because He is faithful and keeps His promises.
b) Personal. It gives us security.

DAY 5
a) Humans lie; God cannot lie.
b) We have found safety; we are encouraged to hold firm; we have a sure hope.

DAY 6
a) Nothing.
b) He knows our thoughts even before we speak or act. Everything!

DAY 7
a) God is just in all His ways; He does what is right and fair; His justice is like the depth of the sea.
b) His mercy, faithfulness, truth; His knowledge of everything.
c) Personal.

GOD IS ... • ANSWER GUIDE

GUIDE TO STUDY 3

DAY 1   a) Holy, holy, holy! The Lord Almighty is holy!

b) God.

DAY 2   a) Great, powerful, glorious, splendid, majestic, sovereign, rich, wealthy.

b) God is in complete control, He is sovereign (dictionary – 'supreme ruler').

c) We should honour Him, obey Him, and reverence Him (godly fear).

DAY 3   a) Shining, dazzling light, light that no one can approach, glory of the Lord shone.

b) They could not go into the temple to perform their duties. No one could approach Him. They were terribly afraid.

DAY 4   a) With God everything is possible. No one escapes from His power; no one can change what He does. He is able to do so much more than we can ask or think.

b) By His power working in us.

DAY 5   a) Everywhere.

b) No one can hide from Him.

c) By calling (praying) to God in sincerity.

DAY 6   a) Heaven and earth will change but God is always the same.

b) God does not change.

DAY 7   a) God is eternal and holy.

b) His eternal arms are our defence and support.

GUIDE TO STUDY 4

DAY 1   a) The Word was Jesus, who is God in the flesh.

b) He was with the Father when the world was created. He became a human being and lived among us.

DAY 2   a) Mary would have a baby who would be called the Son of the Most High God. He would be King of an everlasting Kingdom.

b) She was a virgin.

c) She would have a son by God's power through the Holy Spirit.

d) Discuss the cost of her answer. She was willing to lay down her life for God by the spoiling of her marriage, blemishing her reputation and possible death by stoning.

DAY 3   a) Because of the questions and intelligent answers of a twelve-year-old boy.

b) Astonishment, terrible worry, lack of understanding, treasured all these things in her heart.

c) God (Joseph was not His father).

DAY 4   a) God calls Jesus His own dear Son.

b) To listen to Him (Jesus).

c) Do whatever He tells you.

DAY 5   a) He did not sin.

b) He was tempted in every way that we are; He was tempted and suffered.

c) Call on the Lord and we will receive help.

DAY 6   a) Peter and Andrew were fishing. Matthew was in his office. James and John were mending their nets. What were you doing when Jesus called you?

b) They would have treated him as an outcast.

c) Personal.

DAY 7   a) The teaching of God.

b) Jesus told earthly stories (parables), to explain His teaching in a way people could understand and relate to.

GUIDE TO STUDY 5

DAY 1
   a) He changed water into wine, brought salvation to Zacchaeus, healed Peter's mother-in-law.

   b) Personal.

   c) Ask Him into your home, work situation, He is able to help. He is the same today.

DAY 2
   a) An impossibility being made possible.

   b) They distributed the loaves and fish among the people, gathered up the leftovers, and obeyed Jesus' instructions.

   c) Fear and amazement. They asked, 'Who is this man?'

DAY 3
   a) 'I want to; be clean!'

   b) Jesus was showing by His many miracles that He was the One sent by God.

   c) Personal.

DAY 4
   a) Great glory would be given to God by the raising of Lazarus from the dead.

   b) Because her brother was already dead.
Personal.

   c) Some believed in Him, others made plans to kill Him.

DAY 5
   a) In order to trap Jesus.

   b) They were aware of their own sins.

   c) Do not sin again.

DAY 6
   a) For obeying all these commandments.

   b) His unwillingness to give all his money to the poor; he loved his money more than anything.

   c) Personal.

DAY 7
   a) Jesus called this act a fine and beautiful thing that would be told in memory of her. The disciples criticised her for such waste when the money could have been given to the poor.

   b) By pouring that expensive perfume on His head.

   c) It's not what men say about us that counts, it's what God knows about us.

GUIDE TO STUDY 6

DAY 1
a) With branches of palm trees in their hands, they praised God calling Jesus their King.
b) He is King and yet He humbly rode on a donkey (colt) and so fulfilled Zechariah's prophecy.
c) When Jesus had been raised to glory.

DAY 2
a) A house of prayer.
b) Buying and selling and it had become a den of thieves.
c) Because of His devotion to God's house which burned in Him like a fire.

DAY 3
a) The others gave what they could spare, she gave all she had to live on.
b) We are expected to give generously, cheerfully and wholeheartedly, and God will give to us in full measure, a generous helping, all our hands can hold.
c) Personal. Time, love, prayer, companionship, understanding.

DAY 4
a) The bread represents the body of Jesus broken for us; the wine the blood of Jesus shed for the forgiveness of sins. At Passover, the Jews killed a lamb, put blood on the doorposts and the angel of death passed over them on that eventful night (Exod. 12:1-14).
b) So we don't come under judgment; we need to come in the right attitude.
c) Examine ourselves first. This act of remembrance is for believers.

DAY 5
a) They believed Jesus was the Messiah and He performed the task of a servant.
b) That we should live humble lives, and not think we are too great to serve others.

DAY 6
a) His coming death on the cross.
b) A deep crushing sorrow in His heart, His soul overwhelmed to the point of death, His sweat was like drops of blood falling to the ground.
c) Personal.

DAY 7
a) To betray Jesus for thirty silver coins.
b) Personal.
c) He threw it away, it was worthless.

GUIDE TO STUDY 7

DAY 1
a) He saw what was happening to Jesus and he feared for his own life.
b) He remembered the Lord's words to him and he wept bitterly.
c) Personal.

DAY 2
a) The Roman governor who had authority to either set Jesus free or crucify Him.
b) They chose to set Barabbas free.
c) Pilot washed his hands to show he was not responsible for the death of Jesus. Personal.

DAY 3
a) Stripped Him, placed a crown of thorns on His head, beat Him, mocked Him, spat on Him and crucified Him.
b) They divided His garments and gambled for His robe.

DAY 4
a) They were both condemned to death. One hurled insults at Jesus and mocked Him; the other saw that Jesus had done no wrong and called on Him for salvation. This thief feared God.
b) 'Today you will be in Paradise with Me.' The thief did not deserve this promise.
a) To whoever calls out to the Lord.

DAY 5
a) Sorrowful, heartbroken and devastated.
b) His great love and care for His mother in her situation.
c) Give our lives for our brothers and sisters in Christ not just by talking but in action.

DAY 6
a) Darkness for three hours, temple curtain torn in two, the earth shook and rocks split, graves opened and people rose from the dead.
b) Terror, shock, remorse and hopefully even repentance.
c) 'Father forgive them, for they don't know what they are doing.' Prayer.

DAY 7
a) They asked for Jesus' body, prepared it for burial and placed Him in a new tomb.
b) Because God required a sinless sacrifice to save a lost world.
c) Personal. Discuss in your group.

GUIDE TO STUDY 8

DAY 1
a) To stop the disciples from stealing the body and then telling the people Jesus had risen as He said He would.
b) A violent earthquake, an angel rolling away the stone, an empty tomb.
c) They chose to spread a lie. They gave money to the soldiers; denied the truth even though the soldiers had witnessed the resurrection.

DAY 2
a) 'Why are you looking among the dead for one who is alive?'
b) They did not expect this; they had come with spices for His body.
c) The women believed and shared the good news. The guards were paid to spread lies although they knew the truth.

DAY 3
a) That the Lord had forgiven Peter and that he was included among the disciples.
b) He went to investigate for himself.
c) He was seen by many who followed Him. Jesus is alive!

DAY 4
a) He appeared suddenly even when the doors were locked.
b) Because he had not seen for himself.
c) Jesus said we are blessed if we have never seen and yet believe.

DAY 5
a) Confusion and disappointment.
b) Surprise because they thought He did not know what had happened in Jerusalem. Then understanding, comfort and burning hearts as Jesus explained about Himself.
c) Amazement and indescribable joy when they recognised Him. An urgency to return to Jerusalem and share what had happened.

DAY 6
a) The fulfilment of scripture, and the fact that Jesus was seen by many witnesses.
b) Eternal life. We too will be raised from the dead and taken into His presence.
c) Without the resurrection we have no hope (no life after death). God raised Jesus from the dead and He will also raise up all believers.

DAY 7
a) They worshipped Him, were filled with joy and gave thanks to God (Note in just a few days their sorrow had been turned into joy).
b) That Jesus had been taken up to heaven and would come back in the same way.
c) Personal.

JESUS IS ALIVE • ANSWER GUIDE

GUIDE TO STUDY 9

DAY 1
a) Matthew 28:19. Baptising in the name of the Father, Son and Holy Spirit. 2 Corinthians 13:14. The grace of the Lord Jesus Christ, and the love of God and the fellowship of the Holy Spirit be with you all.
b) He is the Spirit of the Lord, the third person of the Godhead.
c) Counsellor, Spirit of truth, comforter.

DAY 2
a) The Holy Spirit came suddenly with a noise like a strong wind. They saw tongues of fire touch each person. They heard them speak the great things of God in many different languages.
b) People who had come from many countries of the world.
c) Some were amazed but others made fun of them and said they were drunk.

DAY 3
a) Be filled with the Spirit, strengthened, rooted, established in love and powerfully filled with the very nature of God.
b) Our faith rests on God's power.

DAY 4
a) Believers are temples of God because His Spirit lives in those who belong to Him.
b) God shows us the truth and how to live.

DAY 5
a) Love, joy, peace, patience, kindness, goodness, faithfulness, humility and self-control.
b) It is the work of the Holy Spirit as we live close to Him and allow Him to work in our lives.
c) Personal.

DAY 6
a) Apostles, prophets, evangelists, teachers.
b) Practical service, encouragement, generosity, leadership, tender caring.
c) Personal.

DAY 7
a) Message of wisdom, message of knowledge, faith, healing, miracles, prophecy (speaking God's message), discernment, (telling the difference between what is of the Holy Spirit and what is not), speaking in different tongues or languages and interpretation to explain these tongues.
b) The Holy Spirit gives these gifts and distributes different gifts to each person as He chooses.
c) Personal.

GUIDE TO STUDY 10

DAY 1
a) The Holy Spirit shows us what is wrong about sin (conviction) and that God's judgements are right. He also shows us the truth about God and helps us to remember what Jesus has said. He will lead us into all truth and teach us about things to come.

b) Encourage personal sharing.

DAY 2
a) He helps us, comforts us, counsels us and stays with us forever. He is the Spirit of truth who lives in us.

b) By telling us what Jesus is saying.

DAY 3
a) God will give us the right words to speak when we are in difficult circumstances.

b) Personal. We can rely on Him and be confident that He will speak through us if we ask Him.

DAY 4
a) He helps us to pray because we do not know how we ought to pray.

b) The leading of the Holy Spirit is imperative. We need to be praying in line with God's will.

DAY 5
a) To set apart Barnabas and Saul for the work to which God called them. Philip was told to approach the carriage of the Ethiopian who was reading God's Word.

b) God had a great work for these men. They were walking closely with God and were obedient to His calling.

c) Personal. Yes! We need to follow His leading so that we can be effective for Him.

DAY 6
a) Life in all its fullness.

b) God's Spirit gives us life to the full; the thief (devil) steals, kills and destroys.

DAY 7
a) Resisting, restraining, quenching and lying to the Holy Spirit.

b) The Holy Spirit is God's mark of ownership or guarantee.

c) Personal. Do not grieve or restrain Him in your life.

THE WORD WORLDWIDE

We first heard of WORD WORLDWIDE over twenty years ago when Marie Dinnen, its founder, shared excitedly about the wonderful way ministry to a needy woman had exploded to touch many lives. It was great to see the Word of God being made central in the lives of thousands of men and women, then the life-changing effects that resulted when they applied the Word into their circumstances. Over the years the vision for WORD WORLDWIDE has not dimmed in the hearts of those who are involved in this ministry. God is still at work through His Word and in today's self-seeking society, the Word is even more relevant to those who desire true meaning and purpose in life. WORD WORLDWIDE is a ministry of WEC International, an interdenominational missionary society, whose sole purpose for existence is to see Christ known, loved and worshipped by all, particularly those who have yet to hear of His wonderful name. This ministry is a vital part of our work and we warmly recommend the WORD WORLDWIDE 'Geared for Growth' Bible studies to you. We know that as you study His Word you will be enriched in your personal walk with Christ. It is our hope that as you are blessed through these studies, you will find opportunities to help others find a personal relationship with Jesus. As a mission we would encourage you to work with us to make Christ known to the ends of the earth.

Stewart and Jean Moulds – Former British Directors, **WEC International**.